[the summer of pink]

the summer of pink

Editors: Leila Huff and Meghan Nesmith
Illustrations/Cover Design: Abigail St. Claire

to my mom,
whom i love the most

the summer of pink

contents

the summer of pink

This is a love story.

In the past year, tarot reading has been significant for me as a practice of self-care. Each card brings new meaning to different questions and experiences. I turned to tarot as a way to figure out why I had become so closed off about relationships, particularly romantic relationships. I wanted to embrace my path, and live within the memories in order to move forward.

The Beginning section - The Fool, a card that represents spontaneity and naiveté, as we move from the loss of womanhood; innocence to first love.

The Hierophant – deals with the shift in understanding of what love is after first heartbreak; how we second guess the choices I made when it comes to falling in love and relationships. The card focuses on belief systems and the rawness at the core of recognizing the pain that allowed for walls to be built.

The High Priestess card is filled with wisdom and knowledge of self. Having the awareness of what drives one and where one stands.

One final note, it is important to share that the love interests change throughout, but are purposely left unidentified and unstated, because their identity does not matter in the reveal for you - and in truth such things should be left sacred

So thus begins the story,

Gabby

the summer of pink

The Fool

naivete of choice

1.

beige,
the color of the ceiling
that's what i remember
from that first time;
not the heaviness of your chest as you balanced on top,
not you trying to be gentle and forceful at the same
time;
not even what you looked like,
though the glimpse of blonde hair
that dusted your forehead is visibly clear

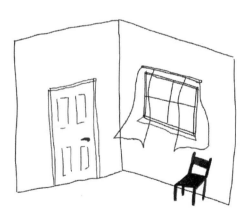

2.

juvenile youth rocked at my core;
snuck off to be held by you
during the days we passed in the hallway,
you smiled, but not in my direction
the pain i felt between my thighs betrayed me,
as if we did not spend hidden among the seats of your van
between school bell rings.
i flirted louder, so you could hear
you never did.
i did not understand
until you asked someone else to dance

3.

the ringing in my ears did not go away;
it lingered there; my screams moved from my mouth to
my head
saying, "love me, love me..."

4.

that night i attempted to forget you,
though you were an idea on my subconscious.
i watched as you were in awe of her and not me.
gulping air, i moved on.
you told me once that your mind was foggy that night,
too.
mixed with liquor and smoke, you admitted that
you weren't in a state to be.
i made no impression

5.

i saw you again.
not being your type,
i introduced you to someone else,
but I felt you stare at me as if at that moment,
you saw what i saw:

my head cradling your hand, feeling every fingertip
against the nape of my neck.

that night, i knew
        roses grow through cracks on concrete
        to remind you that beautiful things don't last.

6.

i once imagined standing next to you forever
the same way we clasped hands in the woods
as the snow fell,
lips close enough to exchange warmth.

7.

frozen on the floor,
grasping at my chest as if my fingers broke the skin
clawing at flesh;
holding my bleeding heart.
the song, faint, but overwhelmingly present,
i cried my hardest that day, and every day since.
listen, you were not the only one who left that day,
parts of me were left scattered,
forever immortalized on that floor

8.

i lasted only a few days, not even a week, or month.
i squeezed in tight corners, breathed in your musk,
wet mouths always seeking the other in the dark
this was what lovers do, or so i thought.
this is how animals behave, i soon discovered,
but i pawed for you each night, and every night since.

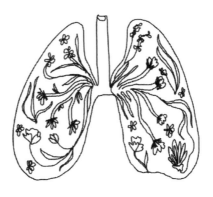

9.

i never told you that i kissed someone else
during the time we were.
i wanted to see if it felt the same.
i blamed the alcohol;
i blamed you;
but, never for once did I blame myself.

10.

why *did* i love you?
why *do* i love you?

was it because you loved me first?
the only one who ever made me feel
worthy of being loved,
but was i worthy of that choice,
                    your choice?

sometimes it keeps me up at night,
until i find myself not being able to breathe,
choking for air, as if air stood still.

the summer of pink

The Hierophant

standing on shaky
ground

11.

i leaned my head back against the wall
i felt my chest rise and fall
everything sat still,
another late night of anxious measures
i was not prepared for how much
the heartache was going to hurt

the fire from my heart spread
up my veins and into my throat
the tiny sparks were felt as they singed

i slowly closed my eyes
and let the wall build
cold to the touch
but protected
safe,
not easy to break next time

12.

there was always a new one
after you.
some i cared for more than others,
some who made excuses for not wanting to be with me.
they hid by the statement that it was my fault,
instead of admitting that their privilege
refused them to love someone that the past would have
let them
take, or rape

13.

part 1.

you smirked as you stood in front of me.
the hiccups from intoxication slid down my
throat, because I needed you.
i grinned back, already pulsating.

addendum:

in truth, you were prettier that me, you still are
prettier than me.
you looked like the boys i used to drool over in
zines that i pasted on my wall;
perfect sun kissed skin, perfect head of hair,

14.

here you were,
into me.
still into me,
but now,
i know your needs
 - and it was never about me.

15.

a decade of what ifs
pulling on the invisible string
that always made me crawl back to you,
even if once in a blue moon.
all for the power you gave me from pleasuring you.

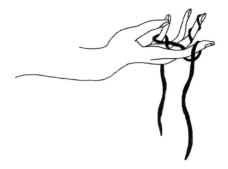

16.

blindly we met.
maybe out of obligation, we were polite
until we connected over heroes in masks.
i wanted to know more; your notoriety haunted me.
i hope you liked me,
i thought too hard about what to say.
you felt uninterested,
then you swept me off my feet, and
i was ready to pounce,
as if, i was stalking all along

17.

i knew i liked you.
our shared fondness for masked heroes in tights
cemented us, briefly,
for a moment.

you were unknowing and
unattainable
like a challenge
        that i wanted to try,
but you made it hard.
most days, you cared less,
then you kissed me,
and kissed me.
then you touched me,
and as quickly as you did,
the silence followed.
it was over and
i moved on.

but then, you crept back in.
now, here, i am in silence,
wishing I never
accepted your terms.

18.

poison is just as tasty when disguised with love,
abstinence is the only antidote

19.

how does one even begin
to find their other half?

if you are lost in the dark,
and they do not know what they are seeking,
then nothing is to be found

20.

i took a chance.
a stranger you were, still are,
but i wanted to be like everyone else;
a risk taker.
someone who could find someone
the only way millennials do.
my patience never got me far,
but then i met you.

i knew what you wanted,
but the heat was tempting me.
i desired you,
it, too.

we spoke antiquity
as we sipped.
the hops lagged on my tongue,
the hand on the clock
ticked on
lips buzzed as the passion
fell on every word that slowly passed
through them.

begotten with chivalry,
you walked me to my door.
it had been too long
that i forgot how.
i pulled you in
as the euphoria of the night,

the summer of pink

nights past
years past
were liberated.

21.

i am not okay
with not being able
to trust the fall.
but if nobody is there to catch me,
why dive first?

the summer of pink

The High Priestess

the anointed struggle of
self-love allows for
imaginable desire

22.

acceptance of
the life chosen
uncontrolled,
managed by destiny
allows for everyday challenges
to feel less chaotic

23.

maybe it was me;
something that needed to be repaired.
what sacrifice of self did i need to make?
was i too much?
did i do too much?
was i not enough?

those feelings always lingered after,
after the first,
second,
the fifth.

until they stayed,
my cross to bear
the heaviest the minute
i locked eyes with anyone from afar.

24.

my delusions of experiences in love,
and in passion
stemmed long before my
femininity blossomed.
i found myself thinking a man
resembled the bare chest cowboys
who grabbed the damsels away from distress.
or the princes who fell for the small-town girl,
who wanted nothing to do with them.
the need for carnal fever the same way,
enticed me to look for my own tale
among the varying men, whose arms did wrap around
mine.
as i grew older, but felt more like vines taking hold,
squeezing
diminishing the same light that i only read
among the pages that now sit in dust
in my parents' basement.

25.

i do not want you for me;
i feel unready,
and undeserving
of having something that
holds such capability
to make one hurt.

i do not want me for you.
if only i could freeze time,
relive a moment
where i felt it.

felt heart
and joy
enter from my toes,
climb through my veins,
pour out light through my fingertips
replay that feeling.

pause it.
don't move forward.

otherwise,
i do not want you for me.

26.

every morning on my side, i awake, one eye slowly
opens, hand stretched, thinking i'll reach out and touch
you there, and just for a moment the sunlight creeps
into my pupil first and your shadow lies besides me,
just like that, we both bask in the sun

27.

dried up.
lack of

                  ecstasy.

craving the moment when
the gasp escaped
but today is not that day

28.

admit it.
fear crept into you long
before you took the journey to heal.
fearing what you think you do not deserve.
rooting itself in cracks invisible to the world,
but most importantly hidden to you.

29.

she stood at the edge,
toes curled on the wood, slightly slipping,
her white dress glistened among the moonlight.
the water reflected itself in the sky,
her hand touched where his hand last mimicked
the crease of her back,
where they danced among
those who smiled and celebrated.
the flower petals followed her,
loose, yet still draping her hair.
the veil dragged on her arm,
torn now.
she was distant,
gone already, but still standing.
this is what she wanted,
but the world hadn't let her.
leaning forward,
the cold wrapped the air,
the sound faint,
the movement flowed
easier now.
she smiled and looked up,
the moon waved away
as she disappeared.

30.

the truth i seek,
i could not find on my own.
the cards directed me in thought
but i desired more.
i needed to accept that i was my own detractor,
a trojan horse among soldiers
closing my heart
from the energy
and the sheer force that wanted to
fill me.

love again, it whispered.

love again...

31.

you have fallen for too long, my child
be present, be free, and in time.
the fear, the truth, the energy,
past and present
will align,
and you will see the silhouette
that has stood before you all your life
attached to only your soul
be with it;
fall freely
love *thyself.*

32.

the compassion that I have for you
is remnants of a summer rainstorm,
still lingering in the air,
gently kissing your sunburned skin.
bristling at the touch as the mist
slowly rises from where it landed.

the aftermath of a caress so sweet
between friends, who became lovers
no longer no more.
breathing iridescent dreams
into a life not yet made–
for a woman not yet truly awaken.
until she placed her toes in the sand and smiled,
embracing her *summer of pink.*

the summer of pink

about the author

Gabrielle Mbeki is an elementary school teacher, who has become micro influencer over the past few years while living in Boston. She has written pieces for a large lifestyle blog, Glitter Guide, and featured on various platforms from The Glossary to Girls Night In. She appeared in *The Boston Globe*, and was mentioned in Step Up Magazine as a "boston blogger that is amplifying good causes." Most days, she can be found with a rosé in hand, trying to find the best angle for a selfie, all while grading her student's social studies quizzes.

You can follow her on all things social media at
@gabbymbeki

Made in the USA
Middletown, DE
01 September 2018